PRESSED FLOWER PROJECTS
Using
Microfleur

I would like to thank the many people who have helped to make this book happen. Bob, my other half, who has helped in so many different ways - a big thank you. My family and friends who they gave me the encouragement to continue. Also the many people who have shared their joy in flower pressing with me. The author would also like to thank the following organizations for permission to use their product names in the text of this book:

Microfleur ™ - W R & J L Beecroft, Caboolture. Qld. Australia

Aristocrat - Photogloss, Goomboorian, via Gympie, Qld. Australia.

Publisher: Jennie Beecroft,
P.O. Box 251 Burpengary, Qld 4505. Australia.
Photography by: Andrew Mahar
Brisbane City Studios

Printed by: Nicholson Printers Pty Ltd
4/16 Aerodrome Road Caboolture Queensland 4510
Phone: (07) 5495 1371 Fax: (07) 5498 3783

First Printed October 1998
Second Printing October 1999
Third Printing May 2000
Fourth Printing August 2001
Fifth Printing March 2005

INDEX:

Forward

Flower pressing is an art which has been practiced for centuries. Depending on the skills of the crafter and the methods used, results can vary from excellent to total failure. The *Microfleur* flower press has been specifically developed for pressing and drying flowers in a microwave oven. *Microfleur* has brought reliable results within the reach of everyone's talents, and most importantly, you know whether your efforts have been successful in a matter of minutes, instead of waiting for weeks.

Since *Microfleur* was first introduced to the market in April 1995, thousands of users have rediscovered the pleasures of pressed flower art. The main attraction is, of course, the ease and speed with which flowers can be pressed with *Microfleur* . Having discovered this, one of the most often-asked questions is "now what do I do with the pressed flowers?" This book is in response to the requests of those many people who want to go further.

The projects in this book are a sample of the many ways in which pressed flowers can be translated into useful and decorative items. There will always be a place for traditional flower pressing and proponents of the art will insist that the traditional way is still the best. It is for this reason that both methods are described in this book. *Microfleur*, after all, is but a means to an end, and that end is to promote the art, and bring it within the reach of today's busy craftsperson.

Over the last three years, I have received and seen many examples produced by *Microfleur* users. Some of these are complicated, some are elegantly simple, but all have created with loving care and a lot of thought. It gives me great satisfaction to know that *Microfleur* has opened up new avenues of creative fulfillment.

All the flowers, greenery, etc. used in the Projects in this book have been pressed in *Microfleur* . They have not been coloured in anyway - they have been used as they come out of the press. Whole flowers were pressed and used whole.

General notes

A flat, dry flower, full of colour is the aim of the flower presser. This can be achieved in many ways including putting the flower into a wooden flower press, a large book with weights on top, and now in your microwave oven using **Microfleur**. In this book you will find flower pressing instructions, some useful hints I have picked up along the way and some projects to get you started.

Keep in mid while you read this book that any time I talk about flowers I also include buds, leaves, herbs, fruit, seeds, grasses, in fact anything you wish to press.

The saying - fresh is best - is true of many things including flower pressing. The best results will be from newly opened flowers with no brown spots or signs of damage. Specimens should be picked when all signs of moisture are gone and pressed immediately. If there is to be a delay before pressing, gently place them in a plastic bag, blow it up and seal, the air helps cushion the flowers and so reduces some damage. Try not to overfill the bag.

Suitable Flowers and Preparation

Any flower, petal, small plant, leaf or part of plant is worth trying, including weeds and some herbs. Some flowers that press well include pansies, hydrangea florets, bougainvillea, lavender, mimosa/wattle. As some flowers press better than others, I suggest you try anything and everything. Flowers with a large water content or waxy flowers such as cacti or begonia do not press very well but with a little practice you will be able to tell which flowers will be suitable. White or very pale flowers need to be pressed as soon after opening as possible, as they have a tendency to go brown in the press.

It is advisable to get the flowers as flat as possible prior to pressing. This can be done in several ways, such as trimming the bulk from the back of the flower, taking the flower apart and pressing the petals individually, or slicing it in half. When trimming the back of flowers be careful not to remove too much as it may fall apart if trimmed too close. With flat flowers such as pansies, use scissors, a sharp knife or pinch with fingers to remove the stem as close to the back of the flower as possible. The flower

can then be placed in the press with the stem beside it. Bulky flowers, such as marigolds, which don't sit flat can be pressed petal by petal or sliced in half lengthways using a sharp knife and then pressed. Rose buds may also be sliced in half lengthways. This way you end up with two flowers and the centre of the bud is very interesting. Smaller daisy type flowers such as the grass daisy can be pushed flat with your thumb as they are put in the press. Trumpet shaped flowers such as jasmine can be pressed sideways with their petals fanned out, or they can be cut just below the 'fullness' and then pressed flat, the hole in the centre will shrink during pressing and can be covered with a small flower to form a 'centre' when being used in a design.

Microfleur enables you to press quite thick flowers, such as gerberas, camellias and some chrysanthemums. These can be pressed whole and will finish only 2 - 3 mm thick after pressing. Before pressing though they need to be carefully trimmed at the back to remove as much bulk as possible.

The large seed pods in the centre of flowers such as poppies, anemone and nigella need to be removed prior to pressing. This can be done with scissors, a sharp knife or pinching it off with your fingers.

Flowers with large heads such as the hydrangea and ixora can be pressed be snipping each floret and pressing separately Flowers that are too thick or which can't be trimmed without falling apart such as sunflowers and some daisies can be pressed petal by petal. A stem or spray of flowers such as larkspur and gypsophila can be pressed whole or individually.

Don't forget to press some stems, leaves, grasses, and also weeds. Curve some stems for interest and also try to get some tendrils from creepers. Weeds and seedlings can be pressed complete with roots for 'botanical' designs.

You are now ready to press your flowers. For this you will need a press, **Microfleur** or traditional, or heavy book, a sharp craft knife, scissors, cutting board and tweezers. You will also need access to a microwave oven if you are using **Microfleur**.

Pressing Methods

Using *Microfleur*

This is a flower press specifically designed to used in a microwave oven. It is a very quick method so although you only do one layer at a time, a lot of flowers can be pressed in a short time. It consists of two platens, two pieces of heavy felt and two pieces of cotton lawn, held together with slide-on clips. To use it - place 1 platen, ribbed side down on the bench, place one felt pad on top and then one piece of fabric on top of the pad. Place the specimens to be pressed on the fabric, making sure they sit flat and do not overlap or touch each other as they may stick together in the press. It is not important whether the flowers are placed face up or down, it is really a matter of what is the easiest. As pressing times vary, it is advisable to press similar specimens together. Also if you have a thick flower in with a thin one you may find the thin one will not press successfully. You can press one specimen or as many specimens as will fit on the fabric. Carefully place the second fabric sheet, pad and platen (ribbed side up) on top of these. Apply a little pressure to the top platen while you slide the clips into place on opposite sides of the platens, so that the whole assembly is held firmly together.

Your *Microfleur* is now ready to put in the microwave oven. Pressing times will vary depending on the power of your microwave and the amount of fluid in the flowers. Lower powered ovens (500 watts) will require longer times than higher powered models (1000 watts). Fleshly or moist flowers will take longer than dry flowers and leaves. Specimens should be dried in stages, starting with an initial burst, followed by as many shorter bursts as are needed to completely dry the specimen. As a guideline, initial bursts should be about 45 seconds for a 600W oven, 30 seconds for a 750 W and 20 seconds for a 900W. Secondary bursts should be about half to one third of the initial burst. Specimens may partially dry after they are picked, or if they are picked after lengthy periods of exposure to strong winds, sun or low humidity. Under these circumstances, or when pressing any specimen for the first time, it is advisable to reduce the suggested initial burst time by half.

Unfortunately, some flowers, such as carnations, have a tendency to burn during the **Microfleur** pressing process. This may be avoided by reducing the number of seconds for each burst in the microwave.

There are a number of advantages in using short bursts of drying instead of a single continuous period:

— this method gives better control over the final product

— where the specimens have thick and thin portions (e.g. calyx and petals) the thicker parts can be dried progressively without destroying the thinner portions

— some rearrangement of petals and other parts is possible while the specimen still retains some moisture.

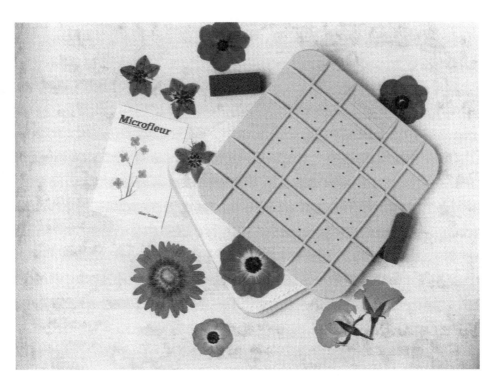

After the initial burst open the press and test for dryness. Flowers with long thin petals, such as gerberas, have a tendency to curl up when the press is first opened. For this reason it is advisable to allow the press to cool slightly before opening. If the Flowers stick to the fabric, gently stretching the fabric should aid in their release. If more drying is required, close the press and give it another short burst. Check again and repeat as necessary until fully dry. Allowing the flower to get cold can help decide if it is fully dry, as if it is still damp it will feel cold and a bit 'squashy'. The aim is to obtain a reasonably stiff specimen which resists drooping and has a dry or 'papery' feel when touched. You may think that the flower is dry and then when you go to use it in the next day or so it feels damp, put it back in the press and give it a 5 to 10 second burst. Repeat if necessary. This can also be done if the flower has twisted or warped due to being left out in the air after drying.

Excessive drying will result in brittleness, particularly for thin specimens such as leaves and petals, and eventually the parts will scorch if the exposure time is too long. Freshly picked specimens will take longer to dry than specimens which have been cut and allowed to stand. Fresh specimens are less prone to burning except when they have been exposed to lengthy periods of strong winds and sun.

With practice it is possible to press quite large and succulent flowers with **Microfleur** including such things as whole roses, chrysanthemums, gerberas and camellias. Because of the amount of moisture in these, it can take many minutes to dry them successfully, but this should be done in stages. "Resting" the specimen by opening the **Microfleur** and allowing to stand for 20-30 seconds between bursts, assists the process by allowing excess vapors to be ventilated naturally. Exposure times should be shortened to 10, or even 5 seconds, as the specimen approaches the final stages of drying. When dry, your flower is ready to use or store until required.

Some microwave manufacturers' recommend that a container of water is 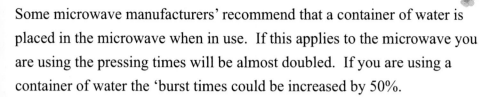 placed in the microwave when in use. If this applies to the microwave you are using the pressing times will be almost doubled. If you are using a container of water the 'burst times could be increased by 50%.

Using a Traditional Flower Press

These presses are usually made of wood with layers of corrugated cardboard and blotting paper held tight with long bolts and wing nuts. To use the press place the base of the press, with bolts upright, on the bench then a layer of cardboard and blotting paper. Specimens to be pressed are carefully placed on the blotting paper, making sure there is plenty of room around them as they tend to spread a bit in the pressing process. Flowers that touch during the process may stick together. Better results are obtained if only one type of flower is put on each sheet. Cover with a piece of blotting paper then cardboard, another piece of blotting paper, flowers, blotting paper, cardboard, etc. Keep adding layers until you have used all the flowers to be pressed, finishing with blotting paper and cardboard. Put the top on, and tighten the wing nuts as tightly as possible. Place the press in a dry, airy position and check every couple of days and if necessary tighten the wing nuts. Try to resist the urge to open the press in the first few days. The drying time will vary, but about 4 - 6 weeks is required. It is possible to reduce the drying time by replacing the blotting paper every few days.

Placing the flowers inside a telephone or heavy book with weights on top is another way to dry them. It is also an idea to write the name of the flowers and the pressing date on the blotting paper, so that you will have a record of what you pressed and when.

Storage of Flowers

Pressed flowers that won't be used straight away can be stored until required. They need to be kept flat and away from light and moisture. I store my flowers in a snap lock bag with pieces of blotting paper, these are then placed in a shoe box or plastic container. This helps to keep them flat and dry and I can write on the blotting paper where and when I picked the flowers. I put each type of flower in its own bag so that it is easy to find when I want it. You could also store them by colour, or in any way that suits you. The flowers need to be fully dry if storing this way, as any moisture left in the flower may cause it to go moldy and then rot. Another way of storage is between sheets of copy paper in a manilla folder or between pages of the phone book. You can also store them in the 'traditional' flower press until you need them.

Colour Retention

Using the **Microfleur** will help to retain the colour in your flowers. We find that some colours change in the press, some reds and blues go a mauve shade, gum leaves take on an autumn colour. The stronger colours, such as the yellow in the jonquil, a red rose, tend to keep their colour longer. The new, young fronds of the maidenhair will stay a vibrant green, while the older fronds may discolor in the press. As mentioned earlier, whit or paler coloured flowers need to be very newly opened as they tend to discolour during pressing. If you are planning on doing a project that you hope will last for many years it is best to choose your flowers from ones that keep their colour well or their design is so striking that colour is not as important. Flowers such as larkspur will keep their colour for years while other flowers such as carnations, maidenhair, and herbs tend to fade after a few months.

Where you store your masterpieces will have some bearing on how long the colour will last. The main culprits are sunlight and fluorescent lights, so if you can keep them out of bright light and sealed in some way it will help them to stay colorful. It may be possible to replace any faded flowers or leaves periodically to keep the color in your arrangement. I have been told that it is possible to paint the pressed flowers with water color paint.

None of the flowers used in tis book have been coloured in any way.

If you wish to test the 'colour retention' of your flowers placing them in bright light, such as on a sunny window sill for a few weeks, will give you an idea of how long they will retain their colour.

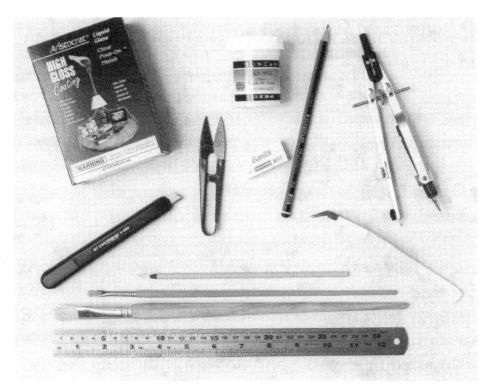

Basic Equipment

The following items should be on hand as they will be needed for completion of these projects.

Pressed flowers - if you don't have the flowers mentioned for each project, don't panic. Any other flower of a similar shape or colour will do, or maybe you could make one up using petals from other flowers. The main thing is to enjoy it, and give your creative talents free rein.

Clear working space with plenty of light - I find it handy to place a large sheet of white paper over my work surface as it makes seeing the flowers and design so much easier. It also helps to protect the table from spilled glue.

Cardboard for cards and bookmarks and sheets of white paper

Glue - Generally I use a good quality water based PVA craft glue and this is sufficient for the majority of projects in this book. A little glue can go a long way so be sparing in the amount you apply. It is best to place small dots of glue over the back of the flower or leaf so that the glue can spread when your work is placed under a book to keep flat until dry. With fine specimens such as maidenhair use a wet brush to apple the glue as this will help dilute it. Try to avoid using too much glue as any excess may seep out from under the flowers and as it dries shiny may detract from the design.

Paint brush or toothpick for putting on the glue - a small good quality artists paint brush is ideal or if the specimen is very tiny, a toothpick may be more suitable.

Scissors - they need to be sharp and come to a small point so that you can get at all the fiddly bits.

Sealer - is a water based liquid available from most craft or folk art shops. It provides a seal over the flowers and helps protect them from damage. It also makes an excellent glue for delicate flowers and ferns, and although it goes on white, it dries clear. It is available in either brush on or aerosol, Matte or Gloss - the Matte is very useful on cards as it is hard to detect when dry. Please check for color change on a sample of card and flowers before use.

Sharp Knife - a craft knife with a retractable snap blade.

Tweezers - long nosed - these make handling the flowers much easier and there is less chance of damage

Cutting board

Ruler and pencil

Pens - a supply of gold, silver and coloured felt pens

Ribbon - an assortment of various coloured ribbon for use with bookmarks and cards

Compass

Piece of glass about 400mm x 150mm - this is optional but I find it a great help when glueing the flowers, also if you get interrupted cover your project with the glass and the flowers are likely to get displaced.

Plastic food wrap - to cover the design after gluing, prior to putting under a heavy book to dry.

Rubber Stamping and Embossing - a great way to enhance your pressed flower designs. There are many specials stamp shops that will be able to help you if you have any trouble with stamping and embossing. Have everything ready before you start - stamp pad, stamp, embossing powder, paper, heat source (such as a heat gun or toaster, not a hair dryer), card. Stamp the design on the card, sprinkle with embossing powder and shake to cover. Shake the excess onto the paper. Holding the design several inches from the heat source heat the design until it goes glossy. If using a heat gun direct the heat straight onto the design, with other sources such as a toaster, apply the heat to the back of the design. The excess embossing powder can be carefully returned to the bottle for re-use.

Two-part Resin (also known as liquid glass or liquid glow) gives a thick, slightly heat resistant, extremely shiny finish on inflexible surfaces, such as coasters, trays, wooden placements, etc. There are several brands on the market, and the one I use is Aristocrat. The kit contains one bottle of resin and one bottle of hardener that are mixed in equal quantities and poured over the project. There are detailed instructions included with each kit. Any air bubbles that may appear can be removed by gently blowing through a straw or with a small propane torch. The process requires patience and a ventilated work area. Drying time can take up to 48 hours and the item needs to be kept perfectly level during that time. Covering it in some way, such as a large box, helps to keep the dust and little insects from damaging the surface. Any flowers, paper, etc. that are to be covered with the gloss must be perfectly dry and fully glued and sealed as any loose pieces may curl and break the surface and then another coat will be required.

Cards

In this section I will give you ideas for several types of cards. Try to collect as many different coloured cards as possible. Some of these have wonderful textures and colours that are ideal for cards. Also handmade paper can be made into cards. In the beginning of the book there is a list of requirements so please have these on hand as you make your cards. I find it very satisfying to sit down at a table and play around with flowers on various cards until I come up with a design I am happy with. I then place it under the piece of glass (before gluing into position) and have a loot at it later. If I am still happy with it I can then glue it onto the card. With complicated designs, say a bouquet, you can either put small dots with a pencil where the flowers will be or place another card on top and turn the whole thing over. you will then have the back of the design uppermost on the the other card and you can glue the background flowers down first.

Sealing the finished card does help protect the flowers and makes postage easier. This can be done in various ways, such as covering the card with some self adhesive plastic or several coats of a brush or spray on sealer, either in gloss or matte. If you prefer to leave the card natural, I suggest you wrap the card with tissue paper before placing in the envelope. If you intend to seal your masterpiece it is advisable to try the sealer on a sample of the flowers and card to be used before sealing the finished card. Seal the card before you add any ribbons or things like sequins, and if you are using matter sealer be careful not to get any on the embossed stamps.

There are as many designs and styles for cards as there are card makers, so please experiment. I will give you examples of some that I have enjoyed, from extremely simple to a little bit more fiddly. These include Christmas cards, botanical cards and 'I'm Thinking of You' cards. Combining pressed flowers with rubber stamps means you can add 'Happy Birthday' or 'Thinking of You' to any card. Or maybe you can apply some calligraphy to give the card the personal touch.

I hope you will get many hours of enjoyment playing around with various designs and ideas.

Christmas Tree

Flowers & Other Requirements:

Fennel or dill for the 'trees'
Heavy white card - folded size 150 x 150mm
Red & gold sequins and gold star

Method:

With the small brush apply a thin layer of matte sealer onto the card to cover an area large enough for the fennel. While still wet position the fennel and apply another coat of sealer over the top. When dry play around with the positioning of the sequins until you are happy with their positioning. Use craft glue and a small paintbrush or toothpick to affix them to the card with the star on the top. When nearly dry cover with plastic and place under a heavy book until dry. When dry tie a bow in

200mm of 6mm red ribbon and glue to the base of the fennel with PVA glue, hold in place with a clothes peg until dry.

Baubles Card

Flowers & Other Requirements:

Red Petals	Geranium
Yellow Petals	Marigold
Purple Petal	Bougainvillea

Really any petals can be used depending on colour preference and availability.

Heavy green card - folded size 150 x 105mm

Spray on glitter, either gold or silver - available from florists

Method:

Using a compass draw 3 x 35mm circles on some white paper. You now need to glue the petals onto the other side of the paper. (So that you can see the circle to cut it out later). I found it easier to glue the petals on before you cut the circles out and the best way to do this was to tape the paper to a window, pencil lines to the glass. This way the paper is back lit and you can see the outlines. Using the matte sealer attach the petals, overlapping them so that no paper shows, while making sure there are no air bubbles. When fully dry, remove from the window and spray with glitter. When this is dry, use a sharp knife or scissors to cut out the baubles and glue into position. For the string either draw a thin line with a gold pen or use thin gold cord. Outline the bauble with gold and finish off by drawing a bow at the top of the bauble.

Topiary Tree

Flowers & Other Requirements:

Small leafed maidenhair fronds

Ixora florets - any small flowers are suitable

Small woody twig for the trunk. It needs to be approx.
50mm long.

White card - folded size 150 x 105mm

Small pot stamp and Terra-cotta embossing powder

Method:

Stamp the pot stamp at the base of the card using the stamp pad. If you
are embossing the stamp sprinkle with embossing powder while the ink is
still wet. Shake off the excess and heat until the powder melts. As the
stem will be thicker than the flowers it is best to glue the fern and flowers
in position and weigh down while drying before gluing the trunk on. To
do this place the stem in position to glue the fern around the top. Using
the matte sealer and starting a little above the top of the trunk glue the fern
in a ball shape. Leave some gaps and have some' branches' hanging down
slightly helps the natural look. It may be necessary to break up the fern
and use single leaves to fill in the spaces. When dry use PVA craft glue to
glue the flowers in position. Remove the trunk, and when nearly dry place
plastic wrap on top and then put under a book for several hours. When dry

23

the stem can be glued in position with dots of glue, placed under plastic wrap with a heavy book on top.

Wreath

Flowers and other requirements:

> Verbena - various colours
> Alyssum - dark mauve
> Small maidenhair
> Heavy white card - folded size 150 x 105 mm
> Sheer green ribbon.

Method:

Place a small dot 60mm from the top of the card and centered from either side - this will become the centre of the circle for the wreath. Using the compass lightly draw a circle with a 30mm radius using the dot as the centre, be careful not to make a hole in the card. Arrange the flowers around the circle overlapping them in places and when happy with the design, place another card on top and turn it over. You now have the design, with the background flowers on top. Using matte sealer carefully glue the flowers into position. Giving one or two top coats as well allowing to dry between coats. Tie a bow in the ribbon and glue into position. Don't forget to rub out the dot.

Blue and Silver Card

Flower & Other Requirements:

> Gypsophila spray about 80mm long with most of the
>> flowers on one side - for this card it doesn't matter if
>> the flowers have faded or not in good condition.
> Navy blue card - folded size 150 x 105mm
> Piece of same card 70mm square
> Piece of same card 80mm square
> Silver spray paint

Method:

Using craft glue, glue the small piece of blue card onto the silver card, making sure it is centered - there should be 5mm of silver edging around the blue card. On the large blue card mark down 20mm from the top of the card and 12.5mm from each side - glue the silver and blue cards in position. They should be 50mm from the bottom of the card. Place plastic on top and then pop under a book to keep it flat until dry. Out of the wind and on a piece of newspaper spray the gypsophila with several coats of silver paint. When dry put several dots of glue along the stem and one on each flower and glue into position. It doesn't't matter if the stem is longer than the silver and blue panel as it adds interest.

Window Card

Flowers & Other Requirements:

Carrot top for tree

Verbena

Maroon card - folded six 150x 105mm

Piece of card 115mmx 65mm and arched at the top, lightly sprayed with gold paint.

Phlox Flowers

Yellow bird sticker

Method:

Lightly glue flowers in position with either PVA glue or matte sealer. Place under plastic wrap and heavy book until dry. Lightly draw a line down the centre of the card and another across the card 70mm from the top. The cross will be the centre of the window. Using a ruler and pencil, on the back of the window divide it into quarters and use a sharp craft knife or scissors to cut the window into four pieces. Glue into position allowing a small gap between them, to give the appearance of an arched window.

Vase of Flowers

Flowers & Other Requirements:

>Antignon Sprays
>
>Heavy white card - folded size 150mmx 105mm
>
>Jar Stamp with gold embossing powder.

Method:

Turn the card sideways and stamp and emboss the jar onto the card. Using PVA glue and a small paintbrush attach the Antignon onto the card.

Mushroom Card

Flowers & Other Requirements:

Mushrooms - I used partly opened champignons from the supermarket. One mushroom with stalk should give three or four slices and I don't peel them. As these are full of moisture they take quite a long time to press. In a 700 W microwave they can take up to a total of 5 minutes of repeated short bursts. Resting the press - see notes on pressing - is advisable and helps in the drying process. As they stain the fabric it is also advisable to use some old pieces.

Heavy cream card - folded size 150mmx 105mm.

Method:

Lightly draw a line down the centre of the card from top to bottom. Position the mushroom slices and when happy carefully rub out the line, leaving a spot for the position of the mushroom. Using matte sealer glue the mushroom slices into position, give the mushrooms a coat of the sealer as well making sure there are no air bubbles. Using the pencil lightly draw the border lines 15mm in from each side and top. Then using the brown pen draw the lines and extend by 5mm at each end.

Botanical Card
Not pictured

Flowers & Other Requirements:

These can be made using seedlings such as carrot or beetroot, or weeds complete with roots. Look for seedlings with interesting foliage and choose the ones with the most root system. With carrots it may be necessary to let them grow a little so they have the beginning of the carrot on them. Carefully remove the soil from the seedling and wash well to remove all traces of soil. Allow to dry or dry with a tissue before pressing.

White card- folded size 150x 105mm

Method:

Using matte sealer 'glue' the sample onto the card, followed by several top coats, allowing to dry between coats. Practice writing or printing the botanical name and then with it beside the sample on the card.

Bookmarks

There are very easy and fun to do and although any flowers or leaves are suitable, it is preferable that they be thin. Whole seedlings make excellent bookmarks. It is something children can make and the addition of fancy stickers or stamps can make these into fun gifts. Covering with clear self adhesive plastic or laminating will give a long lasting finish. Most stationery supply stores have laminating machines and for a small fee you can get the bookmarks covered. It is more economical to take in three or four at the one time as most of the covers are A4 in size. All the ribbons mentioned are approximately 1 meter in length and are optional.

Bookmark #1:

Larkspur flowers - dark purple
Queen Anne Lace (Meadow Sweet)

White Card 150 x 50mm

Dark Purple felt pen

Purple glitter ribbon

Bookmark #2:

Larkspur spray - pale pink

Mauve card 150 x 50mm

Silver pen

Silver & White ribbon

Bookmark #3:

May Flowers - white doubles

Ixora Flowers - Orange

Black Card - 150mm x 50mm

Thin White cord

Bookmark #4:

     Phlox - dark purple

     May bush flower used as centre for Phlox

     Maidenhair leaves

     Pink card - 150mm x 50mm

     Dark Purple felt pen

     Purple Glitter ribbon

Bookmark #5:

     Mushroom slices

     Bone Coloured card - 150mm x 50mm

     Dark brown felt pen

     Brown ribbon

Bookmark #6: Not pictured:

     Large Gum Leaf

     Black Pen

Method:

All the bookmarks are made the same way. Decide on the design of the bookmark allowing for a hole at one end for the thread or ribbon. Paint the card all over with sealer and while still wet attach the flowers. Give an extra coat to secure in position and allow to dry overnight. Using a ruler and felt pen draw a line around the edge of the bookmark about 3mm from the edge, if the flowers are in the way leave a small gap either side of the flower.

Cover the bookmark with adhesive clear plastic or have it laminated. To avoid the risk of the plastic separating it is advisable to leave a small edge of plastic around the bookmark. Punch a hole in the top about 10mm from the top and in the centre.

Fold thread or ribbon in half and then in half again. Fold again and thread this fold through the hole, push ends through the loop formed and pull tight. Put a spot of sealer or glue on the 'knot' to hold in place and trim the ends.

For the Gum Leaf Bookmark there is no need to attach the leaf to cardboard - just write a message on the leaf such as "with love from" or Greetings from Australia" with a felt tipped pen and laminate. No need for a ribbon either.

Decorated Candles

There are several ways to have pressed flowers on candles. One way is to make the complete candle, putting the pressed flowers in the outside later of wax. Another is to fix the flowers to the outside of a bought candle with wax melted with a little paraffin added. I have found the easiest way is to use gloss sealer to adhere the flowers onto the outside of candles. The candles can still be burned, but when the flame reaches one the pressed flowers it may flare up slightly. The sealer helps to protect your design from damage while handling and also gives a shiny finish to the candle.

Christmas Candle

Asparagus fern or any very fine fern
Red petals - any type of flower petals will do
Verbena florets - red stars and pale pink
Purchased white candle - approx. - 70mm diameter and
140mm high
Aerosol glitter - gold or silver - available from florists -
optional.

Method:

Give the area to be covered with flowers several coats of sealer. This helps to prevent the candle altering the colour of the flowers. Using the sealer as a glue place the greenery on the candle first. Then add the red petals, followed by the pink centre flower. Then add the Verbena 'stars'. This can all be done at the same time but be sure to apply the sealer evenly so as not to have any lumps. Smooth out any air bubbles as you go. The design can be repeated on the other side of the candle if desired.

Give the whole design several coats of sealer and if necessary continue the sealer to the top of the candle. If preferred the candle can now be sprayed with clear glitter spray. Be careful when burning the candle if it is sprayed with glitter.

Rings of Flowers Candle

Dark blue phlox

Various verbena.

Purchased Candle - White candle 70mm diameter & 140mm high

Method:

Give the area to be covered with flowers several coats of sealer. Using the sealer as a glue apply the flower bands starting at the bottom of the candle. Give the finished candle several coats of sealer.

Soap

There are many attractive soaps available today and by decorating with a few flowers they are made into very personal and useful gifts. Securing with gloss sealer is one way of attaching the flowers. The soap can still be used with the design staying on for the life of the soap. As some soaps leech the colour form the flowers please do a test first.

Flowers Used:

> Rectangle Soap
> Phlox Flowers and carrots tops.
> Circle soap
> Verbena — dark blue.

Method:

Using the paint brush give the soap 4 or 5 coats of gloss sealer on the side to be decorated, allowing to dry between coats. This will help to prevent the soap discoloring the flowers.

When dry, give the soap another coat of sealer and position the flowers on the soap making sure there are no air bubbles under the flowers. While it is still wet paint another coat of sealer on top. When dry give another 3 coats of sealer allowing to dry between coats. These final coats will help the design to stay on the soap during use.

Trays

Painted or unpainted wooden trays are now available in most craft outlets or you may have one at home that needs a face lift. It doesn't matter if you don't like the design on the tray as we are going to cover. Please make sure though, that the tray is solid, any holes in the base or where the base and sides join will need to be filled.

Jonquil Tray

Flowers used:

  Jonquils
  Black paint

Christmas Tray

Flowers used:

  Various Tree Shaped Leaves
  Thin Metal Christmas stars & Shapes
  Glitter spray (optional)
  White paint

Method: Jonquil Tray:

If necessary sand the tray before giving it several coats of paint, allowing to dry between coats. Then seal the tray with several coats of sealer. So that the Jonquils show up on the dark tray I have used one on top of the other other. When the sealer is dry glue the flowers onto the tray one layer at a time. Wait for the first layer to dry before gluing the second layer, making sure there are no air bubbles. Give the tray several more coats of sealer allowing it to dry between coats. Allow to dry 24 hours. Following the manufacturers instructions mix and pour the resin using a paint brush to brush the resin up the side of the tray. Allow to dry. Using a good quality glass varnish and following the manufacturer's instructions, give the outside of the tray several protective coats.

Christmas Tray:

Prepare the tray the same way as for the Jonquil tray. Position the trees on the tray and using a gold felt pen draw in the outline for the hills. Attach the leaves, stars and Christmas shapes with sealer or glue and give the tray several more coats of sealer and all to dry 24 hours. Finish the same as the Jonquil tray.

Coasters

Coasters are easy to make and make an ideal gift. In fact you could make a range of coasters for use at different occasions, such as barbecues, Christmas parties, New Years Eve, etc. Unpainted wooden discs, suitable for use as coasters are available at most craft outlets. These are available in either circles or squares. Please test the flowers to be used with the resin before doing this project as some flowers are not suitable. Unfortunately wattle doesn't seem to work very well.

Green Coaster:

> May bush flowers - but you could use Gypsophila
> Wooden dice - approx. 95mm diameters x 3mm thick
> Dark green paint, such as Folk Art Paint.

Yellow Coaster:

Tibouchina petals

May bush leaves

Queen Anne Lace (Meadow Sweet) for flowers centers

Wooden dice - approx. 95mm diameter x 3mm thick

Yellow paint, such as Folk Art Paint

Method:

If necessary sand the coaster before painting on both sides with several coast of paint - allowing to dry between coats. When dry give the coaster several coats of sealer. Using the sealer securely glue flowers to coaster - smoothing out any air bubbles as you go. Then give the top of the coaster several coats of sealer - this is to seal the coaster and ensure that the flowers are completely stuck down. When the sealer is fully dry, carefully cover the base of the coaster with tape, making sure it comes to the edge, but not up around the side. This protects the base of the coaster from drips. Trim away any excess tape. The next stage can be messy so it is advisable to cover your working area with several layers of newspaper. Following the manufacturer's instructions mix and pour the resin. Leave undisturbed to set - this could take up to 48 hours.

When set, remove the tape and any drips. Either touch up the paint on the base and cover with glass sealer or cover with felt.

Wrapping Paper

Matching wrapping paper and gift card make any gift special, especially if you have made it yourself. Any thin flowers, petals or leaves can be used. For added interest a few drops of essential oil can be placed in with the flowers and the paper becomes a scented drawer liner. For casual paper, just scatter petals and leaves over the paper or if preferred arrange in a geometric shape. The choices are endless. You could also arrange the design so it can be used as a book cover and when covered with adhesive plastic becomes very durable. Care needs to be taken when ironing the paper as a too hot iron may scorch the paper and if your paper separates it is very hard to join it together again.

Wrapping Paper is not pictured.

Suggested flowers include, petals of different shapes and colours, fern fronds, small pansy or viola flowers, forget-me-not, hydrangea floret, and leaves.

Matching gift tags can also be made using small cards and the same flowers, petals and leaves as used with the paper.

Requirements:
> Waxed Paper - such as lunch wrap (not grease proof paper)
> Iron and Ironing Board
> Several Meters of calico material
> Heavy Cards - folded size approximately 80mm square.

Method:

The method is the same for all paper - Place the required length of Waxed paper on the ironing board - waxed or shiny side up. Position the flowers, petals, etc. as required on the paper. Place another piece of waxed paper, wax side down, on top. Carefully cover with the calico (this helps to protect the paper). Using a hot, dry iron gently iron the calico, which will melt the wax and so join the two pieces of paper together. Allow to cool before using.

To make the gift tags paint one layer of sealer onto the card, while still wet position the flowers and gently paint with another layer of sealer over the top.

Herb Chart

Herbs Used:

Parsley, chives, oregano, dill or fennel, rosemary, basil, coriander, sage, and mint. It may be necessary to thin the leaves of some herbs prior to pressing.

Other Requirements:

Green commercial recycled card for backing - size to suit your frame. Feature paper - hand made banana leaf paper or any textured light weight - smaller than the backing card.

Frame of your choice.

Method:

Using adhesive spray, glue banana leaf paper onto green card. Place this beneath a weight (such as a large book) and leave for a couple of hours until the glue is dry. Play around with the position of the dried herbs until you are happy with the design. Softly mark each position on the paper and where the name is to be with a pencil. Gently remove the herbs and lay them out on another sheet of paper in the same position.

Using a calligraphy pen write in the names of the herbs and when the ink is dry gently rub out the pencil marks.

We have found that herbs such as parsley and mint may lose their fresh green color after 4 or 5 months. With this in mind I only use enough glue to hold specimen in place. This way I can replace the faded ones with fresh ones whenever necessary.

Lightly do the back of the herbs with glue or sealer and place in position. When nearly dry cover the finished chart loosely with plastic wrap and place under a heavy book until the sealer is dry, preferably over night.

Place in frame of choice.

Sampler Picture

The picture shown is 300mm square but the measurements can be adjusted to fit any sized frame.

Flowers Used:

> Top Row - Pink Geranium petals, Tibouchina petals, red
> Geranium petals
> Middle Row - Purple Bougainvillea petals, white hydrangea
> florets & petals, dark pink Bougainvillea petals
> Bottom Row - White cosmos petals, pink Bauhinia petals,
> purple larkspur flowers

Other Requirements:

> Heavy White card   300mmsq.
> Light weight white paper   300mmsq.
> A4 paper or 9 squares of paper each 100mm square
> Green card (or a colour of your choice)   300mmsq.
> Blue tack
> Frame of your choice

Preparation of Flowers:

> Bougainvillea - separate the coloured bracts before pressing
> Geranium   - petals pressed separately
> Cosmos   - petals pressed separately
> Hydrangea   - individual florets were pressed and
>   separated as required
> Larkspur   - flowers pressed individually
> Tibouchina   - petals pressed separately

Method:

Using the A4 paper draw 9 squares approximately 95mm square. (Each exposed finished area is 70mm square).

Using the matte sealer carefully fill each square with rows of petals or flowers - one type for each square, overlapping them where required so that no paper shows through and making sure there are no air bubbles. Be careful with the petals - make sure you have them all the same side up as some, such as the tibouchina are shiny on one side. With the petals I find it easier to start at the top right corner and work in rows across the square. With the whole flowers I pick the nicest one for the centre, fill the square around it and then glue the centre flower in position. Petals can be used to fill in any gaps.

Using a pencil and ruler divide the heavy white card into squares. Draw line in both directions at the following distances from the edge - 15mm,

100mm, 105mm, 190mm, 195mm and 285mm. You should now have an outside border and nine squares with a narrow gap between each. Trim each square of flowers to approximately 90mm square and position them on the card. When you are satisfied with their placement temporarily hold in place with a small amount of blue tack on the back.

Next mark and cut the light weight white card as follows:

On the wrong side draw lines at 25mm, 95mm, 115mm, 185mm, 205mm, and 275mm. This will give you an outside border of 25mm and nine 70mm squares with a gap of 20mm between each. With a sharp knife cut out the nine squares.

On the wrong side of the green card and in both directions, draw lines as follows - 20mm, 97mm, 112mm, 187mm, 202mm, and 277mm. Again carefully cut out the squares making sure that you do not cut through the border or the area between squares.

Place the white card over your design and position the green card on top - there should be a divider of green with a small amount of white card showing on either side.

You can still change the positioning of your flower squares if desired. When you are happy with their placement carefully remove the blue tack and secure in place with craft glue by placing dots of glue in the centre and corners of each square of colour. When all squares are glued down, take the white paper, place small amounts of craft glue on the corners and divides and place in position. Glue and position the green cards on top of the white paper. If you only use a small amount of glue to attach the squares it is possible to remove and replace them in necessary in the future.

Cover the picture with plastic wrap and place under a heavy weight for several hours or overnight. When you are sure the glue is dry, place in a frame of your choice.

Suppliers

Microfleur Flower Press

        Beeline Products Pty Ltd   Tel: 07 5498 5016

        P.O. Box 251   Fax: 07 5497 8200

        Burpengary. Qld. 4505

        Australia

There are Ceramic & Craft Centres in most Australian capital cities.

Aristocrat Resin

        Photogloss   Tel: 07 5486 5361

        29 Tin Can Bay Rd   Fax: 07 5486 5446

        Goomboorian, via Gympie Qld. 4570

        Australia

The stamps used in this book are exclusive to:

        Beeline Products Pty Ltd

They also stock Duncan Sealer, Aristocrat Resin, Cards, tweezers, scissors and glue.

Notes

Notes

Made in the USA
Monee, IL
15 August 2020